THE WHISPERING WIND

Poetry by Young American Indians

THE WHISPERING WIND

Poetry by Young American Indians

Edited by TERRY ALLEN

With an Introduction by Mae J. Durham

Doubleday & Company, Inc.
Garden City, New York

Contents

INTRODUCTION   xi

PREFACE   xiii

ALONZO LOPEZ

Celebration   3
Tears   3
I See A Star   4
Separation   4
Untitled   5
A Question   6
Endless Search   7
Eagle Flight   7
I Am Crying From Thirst   8
I Go Forth To Move About The Earth   8
Dry And Parched   9
Raise Your Hands To The Sky   9
Direction   10
The Lavender Kitten   11

Contents

LIZ SOHAPPY

The Indian Market   15
The Parade   16
Once Again   17
Behold: My World   18

GREY COHOE

Thirst   23
√ Ancestors   24
The Folding Fan   25
Alone Together   26
Mom   27
Snowflakes   27

JANET CAMPBELL

Red Eagle   31
Nespelim Man (a song)   32

RAMONA CARDEN

The Moccasins Of An Old Man   35
Tumbleweed   36

TED PALMANTEER

Hit!   39
We Saw Days   41
Spring Dew   43
This Is Real   44
Judgment   46
The Strings Of Time   47

Contents

DONNA WHITEWING

Love Song	51
The Gathering Time	52
A Vegetable, I Will Not Be	54
Cry Silent	56
Why Is Happy?	56
August 24, 1963—1:00 A.M.—Omaha	57
Can You Can't	57

CALVIN O'JOHN

Dancing Teepees	61
Dirt Road	61
Water Baby	62
You Smiled	63
A Tear Rolled Down My Cheek	63
Speak To Me	64
Half Of My Life	64
Problems	65
Doldrums	65
Afternoon And His Unfinished Poem	66
This Day Is Over	67
That Lonesome Place	68
Good Or Bad	68
Trees	69

KING D. KUKA

"A Taste Of Honey"	73
Ego Swamp	74

Contents

PATRICIA IRVING

Sweet Winds Of Love 77
✓ Going Where 78
Legend 79
You Too 79
A Silver Mist Creeps Along The Shore 80
Sun Dancers 80
Why 81
✓ Goodbye And Run 81

RONALD ROGERS

Taking Off 85
Kindergarten 87
Sioux City: January—Very Late 89

EMERSON BLACKHORSE "BARNEY" MITCHELL

Miracle Hill 93
The Path I Must Travel 94
The Four Directions 95
Talking To His Drum 96

AGNES T. PRATT

Bremerton, January 18, 1969 99
Fishing 101
Twilight's Feet 102
Question 103
The Sea Is Melancholy 103
Untitled 104
Sympathy 105
I'm Only Going To Tell You Once 106

Contents

Death Takes Only A Minute   106

Empathy   107

Fragments Of Spring   108

Lamentation   108

Hope To Keep   109

So Quickly Came The Summer   109

Quietly I Shout   110

PHIL GEORGE

Proviso   113

Battle Won Is Lost   114

Old Man, The Sweat Lodge   115

Song Of A New Cradleboard   116

Child Rest   117

Night Blessing   118

Ambition   120

Make Me A Man   121

Monument In Bone   122

Self   122

Shadows And Song   123

Ask The Mountains   124

Until Then   126

Old Man's Plea   126

Morning Beads   127

Through Dawn's Pink Aurora   127

Coyote's Night   128

Introduction

Because of its nature, poetry means different things to each of us. We move and respond differently to a poem, sometimes in a key that we cannot recognize. The key is not important at first. What is important is that we make our way, although slowly at times, into what is being said.

I am struck by what is said and alluded to in *The Whispering Wind*. The poems bring to mind different thoughts and feelings; there seems to be a trilogy. First, there is the natural expression springing from that part of the American Indian culture from which each poet has arisen. The simplicity of form is present but with the inherent depth of much that is unsaid yet felt. Then, there is the sensibility of the poet who has reached outside of his immediate and traditional world. His new awarenesses and awakenings are joined with what he has known. There is a fresh emergence, a new recognition of himself, of people, of feelings, of things about him. And third, there is the young person, any young person, who has been thrust upon the world and speaks out as a young person might speak out, but with poetic vision.

There is no need to ask ourselves which poem falls into which category. This is artificial, and must be personal. As we read aloud and live with each poem, there is the excitement of individual discovery, of responses which help make certain poems part of our very being. This is the beauty of it all.

That these poems have been written by American Indians is mentioned here only because the culture is reflected. They transcend the culture, and mirror the very stuff of life. I notice, on my part, a welling appreciation of the senses—hearing, sight, smell, taste, and touch. I become sensitive to the joy, the sadness, the frustration that accompany birth, life, and death. At times there is a way of looking that has been almost unknown, or can be rediscovered.

With their youthful yet earthy and lyrical use of language, these poets distill the essence of life as they observe and sense it. They do this with no apparent self-consciousness but in the search for "the best words in the best order."

I compliment the people responsible for this book, for their efforts in bringing to us this mosaic in poetry. What we have here is testimony that human emotion is nothing less than universal. This is gratifying especially in this period of our history.

University of California   Mae J. Durham
Berkeley

Preface

American Indians have been written about from the time of the intrusion of white men on the Western Hemisphere. An indigenous American Indian literature in written form has been delayed by the multiplicity of languages and dialects in use, by the desire for culture protection and exclusiveness, and by an amazing persistence of vast libraries of oral literature.

Here and there, for hundreds of years, an occasional individual Indian has written or dictated folk tales, bits of ceremonial poetry, or reminiscences. Anthropologists, linguists, and missionaries have infrequently recorded and published the personal stories of colorful or talkative Indian informants. Some bodies of the oral literature have been preserved in scholarly quarterlies and historical society printings. The instances of American Indian authors expressing their personal views of the human condition have, until the last few years, been rare and unnoticed.

To understand this, we must know that spring of 1970 marked the first possible college graduation date for significant numbers of our largest tribe, for example. Not until March of 1954 did the Navajo Tribal Council and the Bureau of Indian Affairs and the reservation states enter upon a crash program of education. Only eighteen years ago began the first adequate attempt to fill the 1868 treaty agreement to provide a teacher and a school for every thirty Navajo pupils. The U. S. Government was not wholly to blame for the eighty-eight-year lag.

The People had always trained their children in the skills of living within the Navajo culture. They saw little need for formal, non-Indian education, since they did not intend to live in the foreign environment that surrounded them. Following World War II, cultural isolationism gave way and the adaptable Navajo clamored for schools. In make-do facilities (since replaced) tribal school population rose from fewer than three thousand to over thirty thousand—close to one hundred per cent of school-age Navajos.

Members of many other tribes have attended low-standard schools (both Bureau and public), taught by teachers who expected low-grade work from "just an Indian." In such schools, Indian children and young people were, to their parents and grandparents, collaborating with the enemy. Pupils were under pressure to sit out the time required by the truant officer. They were under no social pressure to learn, to expect honors and awards within reach of others, or to delight in personal achievement.

A few fared better or worse. Many long ago gave up pride in being themselves. Some came, somehow, to recognize the richness within their Indianness. These expressed themselves in painting, politics, sculpture, law, ceramics, and, a few, in writing.

The Bureau of Indian Affairs, frequently criticized (often justly) is seldom praised for its achievements in Indian education. One innovative example is the Institute of American

Indian Arts at Santa Fe, New Mexico—a combined academic high school and art institute. Opened in 1962, the student body since that time has included representatives of from seventy to ninety tribes of American Indians, Eskimos, and Aleuts.

In addition to working for high school diplomas, students study painting, sculpture, weaving, ceramics, metalcrafts, textile printing, music, traditional Indian crafts-culture-dance, and drama. During the first year of the Institute, a few students met with Mr. James McGrath in an extracurricular poetry club. No doubt the quality of such poems as *Red Eagle* (p. 31) and *Tumbleweed* (p. 36) encouraged the inclusion of writing in the arts curriculum.

The superintendent, Dr. George A. Boyce, a distinguished career Indian Educator, assured the incoming writing teacher that she would be allowed ample time in which to draw quality writings from the few students who would elect an art so difficult. He reminded her that Indian students, in cross section, score low on verbal achievements tests. English is, to many of them, a foreign language. Others have attended schools where the intricacies of English syntax are never unscrambled.

At the one-year-old Institute of American Indian Arts, the big question was, Would any student elect to write, when it is far easier and more natural to paint a picture, weave a rug, or throw a pot? This book is one of many published answers to that question.

Dr. Boyce and Lloyd New (then head of the Arts Department and now Director) were more than willing to give both teacher and students time and unlimited support. Mr. Vincent Price provided prize money for an annual writing contest and, always generous with his time and talents, visited classes, taped student poetry, and traveled to Santa Fe to present in person the Annual Vincent Price Awards. He also read our student poetry on nationwide television talk shows.

Magazine and book editors began early in the program to request permission to quote poems and stories. The reading public, it seemed, was ready to learn first hand the Indian point of view.

Students from the Institute of American Indian Arts are playing a large role in the birth of an indigenous American literature. Through writing for others, they are unlocking doors long closed and barred against understanding. Best of all, as they write they are creating themselves for themselves, and are contributing the enrichment of their unique heritage and talents to our maturing American multi-culture.

Santa Fe, New Mexico   T. D. ALLEN

Alonzo Lopez

Alonzo Lopez, Papago, was born in Pima County, Arizona, and attended Sells Consolidated School before entering the Institute of American Indian Arts as a sophomore. His major art interest was writing although he participated also in drama and dance and enjoyed working in traditional Indian crafts.

Alonzo was accepted for an interim year at Yale University when he left the Institute. He successfully completed his work at Yale and was admitted for regular college work, but he elected to transfer to Wesleyan University because curriculum offerings in American Indian Studies at Wesleyan included the Navajo language and other subjects that he desired. He plans to major in anthropology and is active in preparations for an American Indian Festival with an art exhibit and the dance club from the Institute; singers, films, and poetry readings.

He writes: "I am trying to start an American Indian poetry class and the administration is all for it. At present, I am working in the anthropology department, recording Papago for them. It is fun but I never knew that speaking my own language could be so difficult. It seems so unusual to see it written and try to read it, when I'm so used to speaking it only."

Alonzo Lopez

CELEBRATION

I shall dance tonight.
When the dusk comes crawling,
There will be dancing
    and feasting.
I shall dance with the others
    in circles,
       in leaps,
          in stomps.
Laughter and talk
    will weave into the night,
Among the fires
    of my people.
Games will be played
And I shall be
    a part of it.

TEARS

Tears of loneliness
    rinse my memory;
Tears of memory
    cleanse my heart;
Tears of sadness
    bathe my eyes;
Tears of hate
    build up
    to drown me.

I SEE A STAR

I see a star
    yet it is day.
The hands of my mother
    make it grow.
It is a black star
    set against a white sky.

How gentle that star,
Now that she weaves
devils' claws
Together to make
    a basket.

SEPARATION

I wander, alone,
    Through the vastness of the earth,
    Through the changing seasons of the years.
    They come and they go,
    They pass me by,
I who am alone.

Once I was with you,
But those are the bygone days.
    The days of happiness and laughter,
    The days of our togetherness.
We once were so agreed upon a thing untrue
—Two are inseparable.
    Then why am I alone?

Alonzo Lopez

UNTITLED

Go, my child,
   to the lands of your people.
Awaken them.
They have slept too long.
Many years have passed.
Traditions have been carried away
   by the wind.
Old tales have fled into the night.
The way of the Ancient Ones is dying.
Wash away the evil and harm
   that have befallen them.
Lead them in traditional song.
Lead them in ceremonial dance.
Send them forth to the far edges
   of the earth
To find all that has been lost.
Let those among us
   who have left us to die
Know that we only slept,
And now,
We live again.

Alonzo Lopez

A QUESTION

Is it for me to see you
    everybody as I do
    and feel your neglect?
Is it for me to feel
    your neglect as I do?
Is it for me to let you
    dwell in my memory
    as you do?
Is it for me to see you
    everyday as I do
    and hope for a word
    of remembrance?
Or is it for me to cast
    you from my mind and
    end your neglect?

ENDLESS SEARCH

Searching,
    forever searching.
Looking,
    but never finding.
Day and night,
    my eyes roam the world.
Searching,
    not knowing how to end
This search for myself.

———

EAGLE FLIGHT

An eagle wings gracefully
    through the sky.
On the earth I stand
    and watch.
My heart flies with it.

I AM CRYING FROM THIRST

I am crying from thirst.
I am singing for rain.
I am dancing for rain.
The sky begins to weep,
    for it sees me
    singing and dancing
    on the dry, cracked
    earth.

I GO FORTH TO MOVE ABOUT THE EARTH

I go forth to move about the earth.
I go forth as the owl, wise and knowing.
I go forth as the eagle, powerful and bold.
I go forth as the dove, peaceful and gentle.
I go forth to move about the earth
    in wisdom, courage, and peace.

Alonzo Lopez

DRY AND PARCHED

Dry and parched
The ground I stand on.
I sing a prayer.
I raise my arms.
I stamp my feet
And move in circles.
Dust rises
And the sun burns
But I keep dancing
And singing.
If I am pure and innocent,
I can call the rain
From the clouds.

―――――――

RAISE YOUR HANDS TO THE SKY

Raise your hands to the sky.
Raise your face to the sky.
Receive the blessing of the sun.

Scrape, scrape, scrape . . .
What is that sound?
It is my mother grinding corn.

DIRECTION

I was directed by my grandfather
To the East,
 so I might have the power of the bear;
To the South,
 so I might have the courage of the eagle;
To the West,
 so I might have the wisdom of the owl;
To the North,
 so I might have the craftiness of the fox;
To the Earth,
 so I might receive her fruit;
To the Sky,
 so I might lead a life of innocence.

THE LAVENDER KITTEN

Miles and miles of pasture
    rolled on before me.
Covered with grass and clover
    dyed pink, white, and blue.
At the edge of the fluctuating
    sea of watercolors
Sat a lavender kitten.
Its fur glinted from an oscillating
    ray of pink.
Quivered gently at the touch of a
    swirling blue breeze.
Its emerald eyes glittered
And gazed blindly at the lighting
    and fading sky of hazy red,
Yellow, white, and blue.
My heart knocked within my chest.
I must have the lavender kitten!
I ran across the multi-colored field,
    my arms reaching forward.
Time slowed.
I tried to run faster
    but moved twice as slowly.
The blue breeze circled and tightened
    around me,
Holding me back.
The kitten rose and stretched
    sending lavender mist
Swimming in every direction.
It turned and started away
    in huge, slow strides.

I followed and,
    by a shimmering prism lake,
I came within reach of the kitten.
I offered my hand
    and the kitten edged away,
Farther and farther.
Then the lake turned from crystal
    to deep purple.
I looked around.
The colors began to melt.
The red sun turned to dull gray.
The color-filled sky turned to black.
The grass and clover began
    to wither and die.
I looked down into the pool before me.
There, at the bottom of
    the orchid glass cage,
Lay the lavender kitten.

Liz Sohappy

Liz Sohappy, born in 1948, was given in 1969 her Palouse name, Om-na-ma, which was the name of her great-grandmother on her father's side. She says of this experience: "My Indian name has made a great difference in my life. I really felt like a floating body until I received my name. My grandmother said that is how it was to be—no one is here on earth until he has an Indian name."

Liz attended the Institute of American Indian Arts for most of two years and then studied art in Portland, Oregon, for a time. She has ambitions to go to college and study anthropology and attempts to build up a college fund by picking cherries or working at the fruit warehouse near her home in Toppenish, Washington. Since her brothers are on fire control or in reserve service, Liz and her two sisters provide their father's only help for roundups and cattle branding.

Musing on the meaning of her Palouse name, "Stopping on a hill and looking down," Liz says: "I guess I'm a first-class drop-out! A man on television looks at me and says, 'Don't be a drop-out!' Then I turn around to see who he's talking to only to notice that I'm the only one in the room."

THE INDIAN MARKET

Come! What shall it be?
Bitterroot noodles,
sweetroot carrots,
and baby potatoes
for our supper tonight?

Quick! Look about! No one is near.
That tree, that leafy branch,
it blackens my hair, makes it grow.
That other tree, with red buds hanging,
we will drink it for our sweating bodies.

Look! Up there, it is yellow.
Grasp it gently, now pull it slow,
here, into my beaded pouch—
Rouge for our faces,
war paint for our men.

Come! There is work to be done.
There are salmon to be cleaned,
venison to be dried,
eels to be roasted,
and berries to be picked.

Come! Our moccasin prints lead us home.
We will return tomorrow.

THE PARADE

The light glows bright
as the parade begins.
Not everyone has come,
only the old ones.
The Eastern tribes came far,
dressed in cloth, wearing silver.
From the southeast trailed teared travelers
of the Five Civilized Tribes.
From the plains came buffalo hunters
dressed in beaded, fringed buckskin.
The light glows brighter
as each tribe passes.

It was such a long time ago
when he was first sighted,
running through the forest
like a frightened, swift lean deer.
When he danced in bird feathers,
dancing frenzied around blue ashes.
In the twilight of dawn, again he dances.
Drums thunder over creeks
to the swishing grasses on the plains.
Chants echo across the land of yellow maize,
along the paths of the sacred buffalo.

The years flow like running water.
Grasses grow yellow, rocks crumble to crust
as old ones come, they pass.

ONCE AGAIN

Let go of the present and death.
Go to the place nearest the stars,
gather twigs, logs;
build a small fire,
a huge angry fire.

Gather nature's skin,
wet it, stretch it,
make a hard drum,
fill it with water
to muffle the sound.

Gather dry leaves, herbs,
feed into the fire.
Let the smoke rise
up to the dark sky,
to the roundness of the sun.

Moisten your lips,
loosen your tongue,
let the chant echo
from desert, to valley, to peak—
wherever your home may be.

Remember the smoke,
the chants, the drums,
the stick grandfather held
as he spoke in the dark
of the power of his fathers?

Gather your memories
into a basket, into a pot,
into your cornhusk bag, and
grandfather is alive
for us to see once again.

Liz Sohappy

BEHOLD: MY WORLD

Near Puget Sound
when spicy flowers bloom—
red, pink and white—
the wind blows softly,
whispering sweet melodies.
The cool breeze caresses my cheek,
as I lie under grandfather oak
who shades me with his moss-gray hair.

By the California shore
salty ocean mists
shower the sandy dunes
and bronzed worshipers prostrate themselves
before the radiant sun
that warms the grapes to wine
as I listen to the roaring waves
and sigh because the journey ends.

Around Four Corners
when the sun is high,
Roadrunner rests from running
and gopher drowses in the dark,
above him slender grasses grow.
Pine-covered mountains tower
when golden deserts stretch and yawn.
Green valleys throw up sheltering shadows
to hide from frowning deities in the sky
as I lie under a piñon tree.

Liz Sohappy

Over dusty plateaus,
along narrow grassy paths,
rain beads sparkle on forgotten leaves.
Virgin snow beds the earth
and golden nuggets of sand glimmer.
Look at the blueness before you.
Hear the gushing waters—somewhere?
Go, enjoy this world
where to breathe air is life,
as I lie beneath my marble stone.

Grey Cohoe

Grey Cohoe, Navajo, was born at Shiprock, New Mexico, and attended school there and at Phoenix Indian High School. At Phoenix he began to show talent in drawing and in writing. During his two years at the Institute of American Indian Arts, 1965–67, he won many awards in painting, graphics, and writing. He was granted a scholarship and studied one summer at the Haystack Mountain School of Arts, Deer Isle, Maine. Since then, he has attended the University of Arizona.

Grey has been given a one-man show at the university and has been included in many exhibits in this country and in Europe. His etchings and prints are notable for their action and clarity of line.

His poem *The Folding Fan* (p. 25) won first place in the Fifth Annual Vincent Price Awards at the Institute. His story "The Promised Visit" appeared in the Harcourt Brace Jovanovich Adventures in Good Reading Series.

THIRST

What's that, over a distance?
White puffs of gray-shadowed clouds!

Thirst dried my smile—
Not as of sandstorm
Or grit of snow, but
As if it placed a bucket
And waited for a drink.

At the male voice of thunder
My heart stormed with beats of joy.

Slowly blue shadows spread
Over the nearest butte.
Rain approaches,
Wetting its path down the slope
Of our droughty land.

Are my sheep in?
No, don't bother to prepare!
Stand still,
Spread your arms as to worship.

    Rain!

      Rain!

        Rain!

ANCESTORS

On the wind-beaten plains
    once lived my ancestors.
In the days of peaceful moods,
    they wandered and hunted.
In days of need or greed,
    they warred and loafed.
Beneath the lazy sun, kind winds above,
    they laughed and feasted.
Through the starlit night, under the moon,
    they dreamed and loved.
Now, from the wind-beaten plains,
    only their dust rises.

Grey Cohoe

THE FOLDING FAN

The wild beauty of an eagle, once born to virgin sky
    now held in a sacred fan.
                       Beaded feathers
stiffen the grasp, the fingers that curled
to ease the cold soul but let the agony tear,
    for the heart will weep all the same.
Never again is life made vivid
    or for who else the kind warmth?
Maybe this I know, that it is for the dying,
whose ending breaths I hear not, as the wisdom
                    will come no more,
    only to grave, olden with age.
Eternity flies now on the wings of the gone soul,
              never to be seen.

    Listen,
a drum I hear, distance, yet;
        it's from the folding fan.
           The preying bird of death is waiting,
                calling.

ALONE TOGETHER

The tree stands, beautiful and valiant.
    She stands alone.
Now, in autumn, she holds out a yellow blanket
    inviting winter to its folds.
In the snow, she stands slim and tall.
    Her bare arms cry and pray for spring.
The seasons bring her snow, rain, and wind.
    Still, she waits for love.

I will taste her kiss and be merry
    because of her sweetness.
My feet will dance to the drumbeats, rattles, songs
    of the wind in her hair.
Her blue shadows are forever.
    The tree is now.
When the tree is gone,
    the blue will be blown into eternity.
I love her so much
I want to be buried in her shadow
so I can be with her forever.

MOM

I kneel at my mother's grave,
I feel her tenderness at my knee,
And her caress in the whispering wind.
Why can a grave so lonely
Be, too, a place of happiness?
I no longer cry, knowing there's life.
Her heart is in the dark above.
My love and happiness are here.

———

SNOWFLAKES

Snowflakes are falling amidst
    my lazy mood.

Their caressing tickles me into
    pure happiness.

My sadness is buried underneath
    the whiteness.

The silence of the snowbirth
    sets my yesterdays free.

Tomorrow's flakes are yet to fall.

Janet Campbell

Janet Campbell was born January 11, 1946, at Riverside, California. She lived on the Coeur d'Alene Reservation in Northern Idaho until she was ten. After a short period on the Colville Reservation in Washington, her family settled on the Yakima Reservation. She attended Wapato (Washington) High School, before going to the Institute of American Indian Arts as a junior. Writing was her major interest but, at seventeen, she left without finishing high school.

She was married the following year and has one son. When her marriage broke up, she began writing again and won a scholarship to the University of California's Novel Writing Workshop. In 1967 she decided to attend City College in San Francisco and in 1969 transferred to the Berkeley campus of the University of California. She continues to write, but, following graduation, she plans to stay on at Berkeley to study law.

Janet Campbell

RED EAGLE

Red eagle.
Cold, dead, noble, Red Eagle.
Tomorrow they will bury you in Black Hill.
They think you have left me forever.
When I grow lonely for you I will walk
    into the night and listen to your brother, the wind.
He will tell me if you want me.
I will follow the path through the forest
    upon which your moccasins have trod so many times.
I will hear the night sounds you have
    told me about.
I will walk into the valley of Minnelosa
    the sweet grass.
In the white moonlight I will pray.
I will pray to the spirits and they will speak to me
    as they have spoken to you before.
Then I will touch your tree and you
    will softly whisper to me.
From the wind, from the night, from the trees,
    from the sweet grass,
You will whisper to me, Red Eagle, Red Eagle,
    Upon the mountain.

Janet Campbell

NESPELIM MAN
(a song)

Ya-che-ma, he comes,
Ya-che-ma, he comes.
Over the mountains he comes.
Across the waters he comes.
Oh, joy, I hear him.
Oh, joy, I see him.

From the land of Nespelim he comes.
His mother is the sky.
His father is the earth.
He is Nespelim Man.
Oh, joy, he is Nespelim Man.
Ya-che-ma, Nespelim Man.

To Many Lakes he has come.
Let our fields be fruitful.
Let our game be plentiful.
Ya-che-ma, he goes,
Ya-che-ma, he goes.

Over the mountains he goes
Across the waters he goes.
I weep, I weep, for he is gone.
Ya-che-ma, he is gone—
    He is dead!

Ramona Carden

Ramona Carden, Colville, was born on May 9, 1945. She attended grade school at Brewster, Washington, and high school at Brewster and Bridgeport, Washington. She transferred for her senior year at the Institute of American Indian Arts, 1962–63.

She received her B.A. in Education from Eastern Washington State College, Cheney, Washington. She married Thomas W. Wilson, a law student at the University of California at Berkeley and taught second and third grades in Berkeley until her husband graduated from law school.

In early November of 1969, their first child was born—a daughter they named Winona. While waiting for motherhood, Ramona started to write poetry again for the first time since leaving IAIA. "Teaching and the community work I did in connection with teaching left me no reserves for writing," she says.

The Wilsons are to spend two and a half months in Charlottesville, Virginia, for special training and then they will be off to Europe for three years where Thomas will begin his law work for the U. S. Army.

Ramona Carden

THE MOCCASINS OF AN OLD MAN

I hung you there, moccasins of worn buckskin.
I hung you there and there you are still.
I took you from the hot flesh of a swift buck.
I took you to my woman.

She tanned you with buck brains.
She cut and sewed and beaded.
I wore you with pride.
I wore you with leaping steps over many grounds.

Now, I sit here and my bones are stiff with many winters.
You hang there and I shall sit.
We shall watch the night approach.

TUMBLEWEED

I stood in the shelter of a great tree,
Hiding from the wind that galloped over the land,
Robbing, and wrecking, and scattering. It soared.
I was earth bound.
It tugged at the leaves,
At the grass, at things not tied.
At me.
Urging, pulling, laughing in my ear.
I listened but stood.
Flitting away, it spied a tumbleweed
and coaxed it from its roots.
The brown weed soared
and became part of the wind.
Suddenly, with a wild yearning,
I ran stumbling, with arms outstretched.
It flew on beyond me.
It stopped.
The wind flew around me,
Leaving me there.

Ted Palmanteer

Ted Palmanteer is a member of the Colville Tribe. He was born on June 28, 1943, in apple-thinning time near Omak, Washington. His mother kept working until too late to get to the hospital, so her baby was born in a cabin for laborers near the orchard. Her uncle assisted and named the boy for his deceased grandfather.

Ted attended Nespelim Elementary School and says he had bad habits of daydreaming and playing hookey, causing him to repeat the first and fifth grades. He was graduated from Omak Junior High and left Coulee Dam High School for his senior year at the Institute of American Indian Arts. He stayed on in Sante Fe for two years of graduate work in painting, sculpture, and writing.

He earned an art scholarship to San Francisco Art Institute but, according to Ted, his tribe somehow put his request for a tribal scholarship into file number thirteen. He missed a semester of school, but enrolled at Hartnell College, Salinas, California for a year's work toward a sociology major before the draft board called him.

Ted writes that he tried to take the Army in good-natured patience. "I kept in mind, someday, there I'll be on my way to Freedom Land, flying over the Big Pond on a Silver Bird, and I'll sit there and I'll be beautiful.

"As it turned out, after three months of the 1968 Tet Offensive [November 18–February 24] in 'Nam, I was wounded and sent to Japan on a stretcher." The experience is recorded in his poem *Hit!* (p. 39).

Ted spent most of a year at Madigan General Hospital near Fort Lewis, Washington, and was discharged. "I needed time to regain my senses," he writes, "so I worked from June to October in a lookout tower. Now I feel sensible enough to resume living again and I'm a student at Yakima Valley College. I expect to become a teacher in fine arts."

HIT!

I was startled by the knowledge. It was like the last punch
   before you black out and go down.
Like a great paralyzing hand, gripping my body and
   smashing it with a bolt of electricity.

I lay with my mouth open, full of dirt.
My eyes stared at the ants walking over that stinking red dirt.

I felt my mind for thoughts. If I'm to die . . .
I can't remember, but I think my brain has six seconds to live.

I heard a beginning of a shot in strange echo, and a ping.
My head jerked and the ground rushed to my face.
I comprehended a sort of popping behind my left shoulder.
Numbness, shock.
I wonder if that popping was my heart.
Damn, damn, damn, here goes.
I've always wondered how I'd feel.
Disappointed.
Bitch-whore, I haven't lived.

Now, what's this—like lukewarm water pouring on my head.
It's spreading down. My body dreams.
My heart sends pulsating shock waves, white, black.
White! Black!
White! Black!

Damned gook sniper, stick your bone head up,
you slant-eyed little bastard.

Damn! Look at that.
My arm's lying across my face, powdered, a little violet.
I wonder if it's still connected?
Hey, my fingers moved.
It's like mental telepathy or something.

I've got to get the hell out of here.
Got to move my body.
I pull myself and my ammo with my right arm.
I still can't speak, but I can sure think like hell to myself.
You big blond beef, damn right I'm hit.
I'm not dragging around to be a clown.
New Meat, you better start yelling for that medic.

Now I'm pissed. Come help me, man.
I'm too damn slow to get out of here.

Doc, good ole Doc. That's it, pull me off this damn road.
Come on, Doc, save my bloody body from being hit again.

Now I can kind of stutter.
"Unbuckle my belt, Doc. I'll shuck this ammo rack."
The personnel carrier! Sure I can run.
I run, and it feels like I'm hitting my legs on branches.
I look down.
It's my arm.
I look at it, funny like.
I grab it, and I carry it with me.

> Hate! Yes, I felt hate.
> It brings man through.
> It replaces courage and muscle.
> It is life itself,
> At its highest desperate moment.

WE SAW DAYS

I sometimes think of 'Nam and the boys.
We used to say,
"If you goin' to be one,
be a Big Red One.
That's us, baby,
Delta Duds,
Third Herd, man."

We saw death's face
Smelled life's blood as it left,
and death's face.
We knew fear,
Boredom.
We saw days.

The sun pulsated like a huge blood clot
in the artery of the sky.
Consontina wire cut stitches in the clot's face.
Night reached out to ensnare the vision of
        another day.

We hoped with hidden desperation
to live another night,
another day.
We talked,
Passive talk.

Someone told me,
"Don't let anyone push you
        without pushing back, Chief."
I said, "The hell you say."
He said, "We care."
We laughed.
Another night;
Another day.

Ted Palmanteer

SPRING DEW

Now is the newborn time of year.
Tenderly I love its coming-into-being.
Life that swells in buds, swells in my heart,
The kiss of death lies dormant in my blossom.

A sudden gentle lift and rhythm
Turns to eager strength;
A playful, tingling sensation,
Bubbling, babbling, blowing through my leafage.

I can think of nothing newer
Than pure innocence, and this I feel—
The shyness of a two-year-old,
The boundless romping of a fawn.

I must spring into space,
Bleep, bleep at the moon;
Spend my springtime drive against eternity
Then die complete.

THIS IS REAL

And then there was the time I was formed,
Shaped from a ball of mud.
Don't think my thoughts impossible,
For nothing is more real—
I did not remain a ball of mud.
A clear, clean breath of air brought me to life.
I relive vast happinesses when snow falls;
Pure air rushes, gushes, makes me ring.
I ring loud, I ring clear, and people are astonished,
How can one so simple be so happy?
Ah, but have I ever told you who my parents were?
God is my father, Nature is my mother.
And you still wonder?
Through, in, out of this deep knowledge,
I live content;
I have no worries.
Millions of little lights are fluttering in me—
Lights of wisdom, of love, of happiness, of completeness.
These lights glow bright, intense, through living darkness.
Others wonder at this. Lights? What lights?
Friendliness, loyalty, honesty, helpfulness, and love—
These are phenomena we all know,
And still we ask,
What are they?
They are simply here, they happen,
Out of nowhere, out of mud, perhaps.
But they, too, are real . . .
As bright and warm as lights.

They are why I want to live tomorrow,
And the next day,
And the next . . .
Forever . . .
Through shadowed memories, travel flickering thoughts,
Alighting here and there,
Peering into your eyes,
Kindling a soft glow
As you smile.
I feel your warmth,
I live and travel,
Knowing unknown knowledges,
Guided by little lights.
They mark the path toward how to live forever and forever.
For life is real,
You are real and
Overwhelming me to smile,
And still you ask,
Why must he smile?

Ted Palmanteer

JUDGMENT

Here they lie fermenting—
Big juicy, purple grapes of judgment.
Rotten, stagnant, and impure,
For what judgment can they pass?
Must the healthy ripe grape die?
Should he, too, lie fermenting,
Buried beneath this filth?
What Justice is in this sentence?
Its judgment is passed on to infect the vine,
Teasing others to taste and thrive on this fresh fruit,
They will pass from joy to waste to filth,
Purple with pain and heartache.
Dying, wanting to escape this mire and stench,
They are metamorphosed into judges
With fermenting hearts who await in deadly patience
The next small grape of innocence.

Ted Palmanteer

THE STRINGS OF TIME

Passing through the strings of time,
Twinging, twanging, continuously vibrating,
Are great loves and intimacies.
For every creature, every man and woman,
A smile, a tear, a playful movement,
Kissed by the sweetness of living,
Cuddled in the gentle arms of memory.
Yet the tune drones on deadened strings
And all forgotten deeds of chivalry are lost.
Walk softly, dear elegant creation,
For your number now is playing.
Even as you imagine all are aware
And complimentary,
Your great deeds of love and sacrifice
Shall also die as others have died through eons past.
No one will long the melody remember
But snatches of it vibrate on, unheard, yet necessary.
And counterpointed compositions,
Where would you be?
Where would I be?

Donna Whitewing

Donna Whitewing says she was born with the longest hair ever seen on a newborn baby in the County Hospital in Sutherland, Nebraska. This was on May 5, 1943.

Her father was a farm hand and migrant worker during most of her growing-up years. The family roamed from South Dakota to Nebraska. At eleven, Donna was a big girl, tomboyish and bashful. During her fifth and sixth years of grade school, her classmates grew past her and she remained five feet tall.

Donna attended various elementary schools in Nebraska and, on leaving St. Augustine's Indian Mission at Winnebago, received a scholarship to attend four years at Assumption Academy, Norfolk, Nebraska. This is a private Catholic girls' school and Donna was one of two Indians among two hundred and fifty girls. During the three and a half years she spent there, she developed a longing to go to school with her Indian compatriots, and spent her last high school semester at Flandreau Indian School in South Dakota.

She went to the Institute of American Indian Arts as a graduate student and specialized in drama, dance, and writing. She met her husband there. John Vandall, Chippewa, was a ceramics major at the institute. Since their marriage, Donna has helped put John through college and made a home for him and their two children, a boy and a girl. John is now a secondary art instructor and Donna is becoming restless to return to school.

Donna Whitewing

LOVE SONG

Your being has caused
an indelible line
     through the crimson shadows
       of my past;
Over the silent
     white and blue days;
Into,
Merging,
And finally blending
     with the deep dark quiet
     mountains
       of my life.

THE GATHERING TIME

The colored sands run swiftly through the hourglass
    drifting softly down upon the peak of already fallen sand.
As the mound grows,
    so does the empty pit in my stomach.
A twist of the wrist and the glass is again inverted
    I watch the sand flicker down.
Seven hundred and forty-four times I shall invert it again,
    again,
      yet again;
    before this waiting will end
        and I will be able to make a small beginning
    in the direction of my heart,
      my love.

The sharp, searing smell of turpentine in my nostrils,
    the cool feel of it as it evaporates rapidly from my hands.
The heady smell of paints and linseed oil,
    finally the intoxicating feel of my hands and heart
      blending with head and soul
    in search of some fractionated moment
      which I may pin helpless and bleeding
      upon the hospital white canvas.
My heart's memory lurches helplessly against these gathering
                      times.

ZERO HOUR . . .
    still I sit prematurely turning the hourglass
      first this way,
      then that.

Donna Whitewing

Seeking foolishly to cut the hours to half-hours
    then to minutes,
        as I wait for that unseen keeper who will come and set
                        me free
        from the prison of my gathering time.
I do not know if I can fool the Keeper!
By now I am as sick as the girl who waits for her lover's
                      footsteps

    in the moonlight;
        half-dreading,
        half-longing!
In despair I strike violently upon the bars of my memory and
                      plead,

RELEASE,
        to find the bars vibrate a song
          and I have written this poem.

Donna Whitewing

A VEGETABLE, I WILL NOT BE

Who would suspect, or even know
    the ivory-white innocence
    of a steaming hot cake:

Not you?
Let me tell you something.
Wheat grows a pure gold coat.
Grazing is plush green plunder.
Well,
    it ought to be splendid!
Wheat, fed on bones
    for its white flesh,
    ate gold teeth from skulls
    scattered through the yard,
        for a coat.
Green grasses:
    from green flesh at full moon.
Harvesting wheat,
    a man fell dead from heart attacks.
To the Sod!
This hot cake is moist
    and steams of three tablespoons milk—
    from a dying cow.
When time stretches me to nothing,
    read instructions of my burial carefully.
It's all taped to the bottom
    of an oatmeal box—
    third cupboard to the left as you enter the kitchen,
    bottom shelf.
It reads:
    "Lay me low in the wheat yards.

Fill my head with gold teeth.
I could not risk grassing to cows for milk;
Cows dry up sometimes.
I'd rather be a hot cake.
I will *not* be a bowl
  of peas!"

CRY SILENT

I touched a tree
    whereon a Sparrow sat
    and felt him fly away.

The tree followed,
    raising many leaf-feathered branches to
    rustling air.

Then, trembling on my hand
    the tree was solid
    where we stood—together.

Walking away,
    "I might come again
    to touch
    that tear-streaked bark,"
        I thought.

———

WHY IS HAPPY?

I cried because I didn't have
A little bitty slice of something else;
Then the sun reached down
    and tickled my tears—
I made a laughing bowl
    that caught the tears
To wash the hand that touched me.

56

Donna Whitewing

AUGUST 24, 1963—1:00 A.M.—OMAHA

Heavy breathing fills all my chamber
Sinister trucks prowl
    down dim-lit alleyways.
Racing past each other,
    cars toot obscenities.
Silence is crawling in open windows
    smiling and warm.
Suddenly,
    crickets and cockroaches
    join in the madness:
    cricking and crawling.
Here I am!
A portion of some murky design.
Writing,
    because I cannot sleep,
    because I could die here.

————

CAN YOU CAN'T

Take a wooden doll,
    split its wooden heart.
Fill the cavity
    with dry leaves
    and dusty feathers.
Glue it back together.

Calvin O'John

Calvin O'John, Ute-Navajo, was born in Denver, Colorado, on November 24, 1946. He attended grade school at Ignacio, Colorado, and did his high school work at the Institute of American Indian Arts. He was graduated in 1967.

Calvin's paintings—boldly stylized—stand in stark contrast to his wide-eyed, childlike writing style. His paintings were widely exhibited from the Institute and lauded by such authorities as the curator of the Museum of Modern Art in New York. Many examples of his work are retained in the permanent gallery collection at the Institute.

Since graduation, Calvin has been living in Oakland, California, trying to find his niche in the world. He has received training in various fields, from cookery to bank telling, none of which challenge his sensitivity or give him scope for expression of his simple, fundamental appreciations. A long siege with hepatitis has complicated his getting on with the business of living.

He writes: "San Francisco is something else! I get with the wrong bunch on the wrong side of town, but I still love the city. It's so pretty! At times I go down by the Lake here in Oakland and sit there, thinking of my mother, of IAIA and my friends, and trying to write poems, but I just can't get started."

Calvin O'John

DANCING TEEPEES

Dancing teepees
High up in the Rocky Mountains,
Dancing teepees
Dance on the grassy banks of Cripple Creek
With laughing fringes in the autumn sun.
Indian children
Play with bows and arrows
On the grassy banks of Cripple Creek.
Indian women
Gather kindling
To start an evening fire.
Dancing teepees
Dance against fire-lighted autumn trees.
Braves returning
Home from raiding,
Gallantly ride into camp
With horses, scalps, and ornaments.
Dancing teepees
Sleep now on the grassy banks of Cripple Creek
High up in the Rocky Mountains.

DIRT ROAD

A shiny stone by a dirt road
So small, yet so beautiful
I picked it up. So beautiful it was
    I put it down
        And walked on.

Calvin O'John

WATER BABY

In the thick shallow streams
there lives a water baby.
The baby of the streams,
    I call it.
So small you are, water baby,
A baby without a mother!
Where is your mother?
    Is she dead?
I pity you, water baby,
having to live in the shallow streams,
So cold on winter days and nights,
But so warm and beautiful in summer days.

I once saw you from a distance,
    but that was all.
Other people who have seen you
    threw stones at you.
How cruel they are!
Oh, water baby, go away from
    the shallow streams.
Head toward the sea, water baby,
    And find your mother.
        Go, water baby.

YOU SMILED

You smiled,
I smiled,
So we're both happy,
But deep down inside
There is hatred between us.
Let's not show our inside feeling
      to one another;
        Just keep on smiling
        Until we smile away our hate.

———

A TEAR ROLLED DOWN MY CHEEK

A tear rolled down my cheek
And more came down
Until tears rolled down like a stream.
My eyes were blind with tears for you.
They washed my eyes till I could see.

63

SPEAK TO ME

Oh trees, say something.
One day you move back and forth,
Another day you are still.
How can I tell
What you are thinking, feeling?
Please speak to me.
Lovers carve names in you.
That must be painful.
I sit beneath your branches on sunny days,
When the wind blows and
Your leaves whisper and fly away,
Waiting for you to speak to me.
Are you angry at everybody?
Do you feel pain or delight?
Oh trees, please speak to me.

———

HALF OF MY LIFE

Half of my life
I've wasted on you.
Half, dead and buried beneath memories;
Half, waiting for someone new.
Trembling, my other half waits.

Calvin O'John

PROBLEMS

The end of the day is near.
Gather up your problems
for this day.
Keep some,
Throw some away.

———

DOLDRUMS

A little dog
That walks in the field—
Everywhere he goes
His head slumps down and
He's not waggling his tail any more—
A little dog
That nobody wants.

Calvin O'John

AFTERNOON AND HIS UNFINISHED POEM

Afternoon sits down on an old rocking chair
and starts writing his poem.
The sun drops by and adds a
few bright words.
All is going well.
Then, unexpectedly,
out of the gray sky
comes wind, his huge cheeks puffed up.
He lets out a burst that carries
Afternoon's unfinished poem
across the corn fields.
Afternoon is angry.
He gets up from the old rocking chair
and chokes wind's throat so he can't
blow any more.
The wind dies down.
Afternoon goes and searches
for his unfinished poem.

Calvin O'John

THIS DAY IS OVER

When the day is over,
I think of all I did.
Did I goof off,
Or did I accomplish something?
Did I make a new friend,
Or did I make an enemy?
Was I mad at everybody,
Or was I nice?
Anyway, what I did today is over.
While I sleep,
The world will be shining up
A new day for me to use,
Or goof up,
Or whatever I decide
To do with it.
Tonight, I pick out
"Nice," and
"Friendly," and
"Accomplish something."

Calvin O'John

THAT LONESOME PLACE

That lonesome path that leads to Nowhere
Is taking me away from this lonesome place.

———

GOOD OR BAD

Good or bad,
By tomorrow I will have
Changed something—
Myself, perhaps.
Maybe?
No, for sure.

Calvin O'John

TREES

The trees walked
along the mountainside.
Against the sunset,
I see them dancing
with one another.
I run after them
but they run faster.
I dance myself against
the sunset.
Exhausted, I fall.
The trees trample me.
The sun has set.
The trees walk on.

King D. Kuka

King Kuka was born on August 13, 1946, at Browning, Montana. He is a member of the Blackfeet Tribe. He attended Valier High School, Valier, Montana, during his freshman and sophomore years. He transferred in 1963 to the Institute of American Indian Arts and was graduated in 1965. During high school, he played basketball and football and was voted Most Valuable Basketball Player at IAIA. He studied painting, sculpture, and creative writing and won honors for achievements in all three fields.

In writing, he won wide recognition for poetry, short stories, and legends. He has exhibited and won prizes in painting and sculpture shows in New York; San Francisco; Tulsa; Washington, D.C.; Anchorage, Alaska; Ankara, Turkey; Edinburgh, Scotland; Berlin; and throughout Montana, Wyoming, Utah, and Arizona.

King spent two years in military service, serving in Company D., 16th Signal Battalion in Butzbach, Germany. Since separation, he has completed his freshman year at the University of Montana with a major in fine arts.

King D. Kuka

"A TASTE OF HONEY"

True: nor love or loving is ultimate.
A doe, free in the valley,
    that but her head concealed by green,
    hoofs cleansed by artesian waters,
Is harnessed by love that shuns her.
While beauty slumbers, tonight love travels afar.

Love is nay but thatching in storm,
    for a wind tears damp and cold,
    cruel and ruthless.
A fallen traveler like weather-beaten gaff
    shall sink, rise, sink, rise, thrice sink,
    rise ne'r from love experienced in icy depths.
The thickened lung is so with breath,
Not satisfaction of love.

Love is peace, yet it is mortal.
Plead release.
Console yourself with sorrow;
Tantalized you shall be by love.
Treasure love's memory.
Sell it to tears, regret, self-pity.
Love's outstretched arms seek to destroy you.

Love is the venom of a reptile;
A wasp, fitter to kill than keep.
Within the venom dwells death;
Without is honey.
Gamble carelessly venom's deadly game
    and you'll be dealt a losing hand.
Carefully give, and in return
Will be "a taste of honey."

EGO SWAMP

Fool be he who walks my track
Midst a dark of dampened hush and fog.
Ha! Ha! Track to swamp and him to doom.
Bog, mire, smother and spare not his soul.

Ego ensnares him in a sticky web of boast.
Conceit, complacence, confidence. Deep are the tracks.
Deep and deeper then he sinks. A most secure foothold!
Ego Swamp soon for him has debt unpaid.

Nearer . . . Unsure steps now. Hark!
  Cricket snaps, "Forbidden."
Slowly! Listen . . . Toad's deathly gasp!
  Heart drums fear!

No. Yet, yes. Too late! True, he is enspun
And Ego's cunning snicker . . . "I've got you!"

Patricia Irving

Patricia Irving's first memories are of foster homes. Her mother contracted tuberculosis and was "away" for three years—until little "Pat" was five. When her mother finally recovered, she was ecstatic for a few months, but then sister Betsy arrived and Pat again found herself alone and lonely. Frequent moves from Neah Bay to Seattle to Port Angeles and back to Neah Bay kept Patricia school hopping all through the grades. From her eighth to tenth grades, she lived in another foster home and attended West Seattle High School.

In the fall of her sixteenth year, Pat transferred to the Institute of American Indian Arts. She spent two happy years in Santa Fe, but returned to Neah Bay before graduating. Her plan to attend Western Washington State College was disrupted by the birth of a son, Barry Alan, but she has continued to write even while earning her living at various kinds of employment in and around Seattle.

Patricia Irving

SWEET WINDS OF LOVE

Sweet winds of love, sweep not my plains
    for bitter darkness soon would fall
The clouds would come and sadden all
    with cold, dark rains—
And you, sweet winds, would leave to blow
    the distant plains
        in distant lands,
            and nevermore return.

Sweet winds of love, sweep not my plains
    for love
        and pain
           are one.

'Tis true, sweet winds,
    a rainbow would ensue the storm,
But even rainbows wear tints of
    blue
        and gray
          and black.

Patricia Irving

GOING WHERE

Yesterday brings dreams of rain.
　　Tearlit, moonlit silver pain.
Youth's sweet years are flying fast.
　　Winds of love cry in the past.

Youth is fading—going where?
　　Going where the winds don't care.
Yesterday brings dreams of rain.
　　Tearlit, moonlit silver pain.

Youth is standing on the beach,
　　Laughing at me—out of reach.
Youth is fading—going where?
　　Going where the winds don't care.

Youth's now woman, standing proud.
　　Yesterday's a misty cloud.
Youth is fading—going where?
　　Going where the winds don't care.

LEGEND

Sleep, legend, but call me when you wake.
    Your people call, yet hear no answer.

I beg you, legend, heed the call
    Before it is too late.

A tale may die on restless lips, but,
    Legend, wake and say you slept.

YOU TOO

Dewy drops
wear down
rock-hard ambition,
pound it to particles
washed downstream
with broken promises
to self
and brittle dreams.
Delight in dewdrops.

Patricia Irving

A SILVER MIST CREEPS ALONG THE SHORE

A silver mist creeps along the shore
    and threads among the priestly pines.
And this shall be, forevermore.

————

SUN DANCERS

Sun dancers
Whirling, twirling madly—
Feet churning Mother Earth
Until clouds weep.

Sun dancers
Bringing song to life
With forlorn drumbeat,
With feathers bright.

Sun dancers'
Feathers bowing to four winds,
Feathers dampened by the rain;
Corn feathering on the stalk.

Sun dancers
Throw humble gratitude to sky
In thundering beat
From whirling, churning feet.

Patricia Irving

WHY

Where do I look?
What book,
On what shelf
Tells why I am?

———————

GOODBYE AND RUN

A brief goodbye—
vague
yet all too final.
Making naked wishes
to the breeze,
she runs,
trying to outrun
her tears.

Ronald Rogers

Ronald Rogers was born on November 20, 1948, at the Indian Hospital at Claremore, Oklahoma. He is a member of the Cherokee Nation. He lived with his parents in Oklahoma City until he was three or four. After that, he was shunted from orphanage to orphanage and attended public schools in Oklahoma City and Wichita.

At fifteen, he entered the Institute of American Indian Arts as a sophomore. His major interest became writing, particularly short stories. He also developed an aptitude for drama and acted several major roles in school and community performances.

In his junior year at IAIA, Ron won a second place in the nationwide Scholastic Awards and his short story, "The Good Run," appeared in *Cavalcade* magazine for January 1967. August Derleth, one of the contest judges, said of this story: "The Good Run" is clearly the product of skill, perception, and discipline; the story is well conceived, well ordered, effective." (*Cavalcade*, May 1966.)

Ron attended San Francisco State College during the 1968–69 Hayakawa-hiatus year, wrote on his own one term, and transferred mid-term, 1970, to UCLA.

Ron's favorite format for writing continues to be the short story, but poetry serves him in the kind of escape-valve capacity that produces an occasional deceptively simple poem.

Ronald Rogers

TAKING OFF

1
Barely did the dust settle
huddle down
than the wind blew
kicked it up
slapped me right in the eyes.

"Oh, hell," I said.

2
The dust sits on everything
everyone
on the streets
on everyone
I blow (whew)
to clean them off.

They cloud up.

3
I stuff my bag
full of clothes
the road is dusty
the road sign is dusty
my thumb is dusty
I blink.

Somebody gives me a ride.

4
The car starts up
we're off
the road is smooth
zump zump zump
go the white paint lines
beneath us.

I feel superior.

5
The driver asks me
"Where are you going?"
"Beg pardon?" I say.
The driver laughs
slaps my back
the dust blooms up
I cough.

I tell him to stop the car.

6
I am sitting on my bag
I sigh
I put out my thumb
zzzzem
goes a car.

The dust swirls up.

KINDERGARTEN

In my kindergarten class
there were windows around the room
and in the morning we all took naps.
We brought our own rugs and crayons
because that was responsibility
and we learned to tell the colors apart.

Sometimes we read stories
about wrinkled old pirates with parrots
who talked about cities of gold.
And then we'd talk about cities of gold
with streets of silver
and we'd laugh and laugh and laugh.

The floors were all made of wood
in long, long strips—
brown wood with fun-peely wax.
One day the toughest kid in school
got mad and yelled at the teacher
and we smiled when he went to the principal.

The principal had a long black whip
studded through with razor blades
and nine lashes on it.
The principal wore a black suit
and smoked Pall Malls
and wrote bad notes to your father.

In my kindergarten class
there were windows around the room
and in the morning we all took naps.
We brought our own rugs and crayons
because that was responsibility
and we learned to tell the colors apart.

Ronald Rogers

SIOUX CITY: JANUARY—VERY LATE

I have listened for this and that
in odd hotel rooms
in odder   concrete towns
to the tune of
radiator rattle   a dog-bark distant

Watched for it in
newspapers folded   on the floor
in library books   by James Baldwin
a bed sheet tangled   against the wall

Smelled it
in round bowls of
last-minute oatmeal
on dusty plates
instant coffee in flowered cups

I can only conclude:
radiator   headlines   breakfast.

Emerson Blackhorse
"Barney" Mitchell

Barney Mitchell's home is near Shiprock, New Mexico. He was born in a hogan on March 3, 1945. He attended school at Ignacio, Colorado, until his junior year in high school when he transferred to the Institute of American Indian Arts. His father had died in service in World War II. His maternal grandparents cared for him and gave him his early training in the Navajo way.

At the Institute, he did not care for any of the arts until he discovered writing, but writing in English presented almost insurmountable difficulties. His own unique sensitivity and his honest struggle to put on paper his sensory experience kept shining through his tangled grammar, however. For two years he wrote the story of his childhood and growing-up years on the reservation, revealing much of human interest about the Navajo people and about his own determination to gain an education. As *Miracle Hill*, this story was published in 1967 by the University of Oklahoma Press.

The poem *Miracle Hill* (p. 93) provided the title for the book and pinpoints its theme.

Barney attended Fort Lewis College, Durango, Colorado, for one year and transferred to Navaho Community College, Many Farms, Arizona, where he continues with his college work and is, also, an assistant to the president and a teaching associate.

MIRACLE HILL

I stand upon my miracle hill,
    Wondering of the yonder distance,
Thinking. When will I reach there?

I stand upon my miracle hill.
    The wind whispers in my ear.
I hear the songs of old ones.

I stand upon my miracle hill.
    My loneliness I wrap around me.
It is my striped blanket.

I stand upon my miracle hill
    And send out touching wishes
To the world beyond hand's reach.

I stand upon my miracle hill.
    The bluebird that flies above
Leads me to my friend, the white man.

I come again to my miracle hill.
    At last, I know the all of me—
Out there, beyond, and here upon my hill.

THE PATH I MUST TRAVEL

Within the curved edge of quarter moon
    I was told there is a road
I must travel to meet the divine one,
    On this glittering crescent.

Awed, I tremble, enfolding tobacco
    The Almighty has given us,
To put forth our faith prayers
    Rolled in the precious smoke.

I wait in patience for the light,
    Gazing at glowing galaxies
Beyond the curve of risen silver bow.
    Silent, I sit listening.

Before me I see wrinkled old man,
    Torch in his right hand for me.
I breathe in burning leaf smoke.
    I hear waterdrum and a rattle.

Fasting through the long hours,
    I stand before the universe.
I hold forth my hands four times,
    I see the Mighty One!

Within the whirling mist smoke,
    The drifting scent of cedar,
The fluffy eagle feather waked me.
I step out into blinding space.

Emerson Blackhorse "Barney" Mitchell

THE FOUR DIRECTIONS

A century and eight more years,
     Since Kit Carson rode from four directions,
Deep into the heart of nomadic Navajos,
     Burning, ravishing the Land of Enchantment.

Prairie grasses are once more
     Growing as high as the horse's belly.
Cradles of wrapped babies in colors
     Of the rainbow again span the land.

I know my people will stand and rise again.
     Now it is time.
Pollen of yellow grain,
     Scatter in the four directions.

TALKING TO HIS DRUM

When first glow of early dawn
    Comes peering over blackened mesas,
Appears from hogan, wrinkled, gray-haired man.

In the midst of quivering light rays
    Golden orb winks up
To greet and warm enchanting old one.

Leaning on his cane he stands forth,
    Fasts until the time has come
To sing his song of glory yet to be.

Hollow drum, goat hide stretched across it,
    He holds within the circle of his arm;
Lays his ear upon it, listens.

Now he beats out protestations
    In chattering and whispers,
Chanting long-unheeded, long-forgotten myths.

The people listen but cannot understand
    Only Great Spirit of the Universe
Hears him, talking to his drum.

Agnes T. Pratt

Agnes T. Pratt, Suquamish, was born at Bremerton, Washington, on December 23, 1945. She attended North Kitsap Elementary School at Poulsbo, Washington and three different high schools: North Kitsap; St. Euphrasia High, Seattle, Washington; and the Institute of American Indian Arts, Santa Fe, New Mexico. She stayed on at the Institute for two years of graduate work.

She arrived at the Institute with no language problems, having learned English as her first language, but she happened into writing classes by the process of feeling no interest in the other art offerings. She chose painting as a second art class by the same process and became highly adept as a colorist.

She spent the summer of '69, teaching in the Head Start program at Suquamish and says, "Helping disadvantaged preschoolers prepare for school was one of the most enjoyable experiences of my life."

She is now attending Olympic Junior College, Bremerton, Washington, and hopes to make teaching her profession. Lamenting her slowness in getting through school, she writes, "But I'm still young enough to pick red-purple clovers and give them to my friends in bunches, for I know they like expensive things."

BREMERTON, JANUARY 18, 1969

Blank faces full of eyes
turn toward the business
of asking who are you.
A line of them, of people
sit hunched against the bar counter
drinking schooners of beer
counting minutes, asking the clock,
asking you.
I do not know.

There is only one place to sit.
I sit down, look around
and ask them.
A pressure of a body
leans against me
He is neither young nor old
face well masked in tired drunkenness
a curly mustache and a beard
out of one coat sleeve
a steel hook where a hand should be
he sits, silent.
Then, leans over drunkenly
and asks
Are you looking for a place to hide?

I laugh a small laugh
Indulgently—
and almost—
Almost tell him no,
I am not looking for a place to hide
for I am already well-hidden.

On the counter in front of him
are two brown bags
two bottles of wine.

He stands up, sticks one inside his coat
turns toward me and asks
Would you like to go with me?
No.

He turns and I hear a crash, shattering
of glass and wine sticky stench
floats up
"Damn." "Broke my bottle of Logey."
The barmaid flutters up
gives him the mean you-rummy look.
He swears. Throws the other bottle
across the floor in front of her
turns, saunters out the door.

A real hero, everyone says.
He's a real hero

He has let go
and they wipe up the mess
with misunderstanding.

Midnight and we are all well-hidden.

FISHING

Grandfather and the oars are one body,
Thrusting the boat forward.
Jess and I peer downward in child-fear
For the wake is a wide, waiting, child-eating jaw.
An oar splash becomes an echo
That shivers across the waves.
We are abandoned, grandfather and the boat
A faraway security.
Round-eyed words whisper from us.
Grandfather half turns and we are silent;
We must be very quiet
Or we will scare the fish away.

Agnes T. Pratt

TWILIGHT'S FEET

In corridors and caverns of my memory,
I shall run forever along pine-shaded paths,
Wild woodland paths,
    bordering the wilder, lonelier sea!
Forever I'll hear gray sea gulls
Laugh and wheel, rumpling the salt sea air.
Forever I'll sigh when I see the sun
    smile through feather-needled pine trees.
Forever I'll watch the fog mists
Creep through silenced dark,
    slipping among the trees,
    following twilight's feet.
Forever I'll run and feel the splash of rain,
Liquid fingers,
    reaching down to join sad skies and me.

In corridors and caverns of my memory
I shall run forever along pine-shaded paths,
Paths lonely, except that
Twilight in her veil of friendly fog
Runs with me.

QUESTION

Whence the beginning?
Whence the end?
At what hour did I hear you call?
At what hour did I stop listening?
Answer, heart that built a wall!

THE SEA IS MELANCHOLY

As sad and salt as tears,
The sea is melancholy.

It sings a song its mystic own,
The minor, melancholy sea.

Listen! Hear its Orphean melody,
Lamentations of the sea.

Coaxing, luring, nudging me
To run barefoot toward joy.

Agnes T. Pratt

UNTITLED

I've built myself a stairway.
All my yesterdays
Are steps ascending;
They try to touch my sky,
But they'll never reach it,
      My stairway is a lie.

I'm going to wash my face
With your sunny smiles
And borrow the twinkle in your eyes.
You'll be there in the mirror's reflection;
      ME—in disguise!

Agnes T. Pratt

SYMPATHY

Into his pool of silent sorrow
My words fall like heavy stones
Striking, splashing, and shattering
The tranquilness of his pool of tears,
Afflicting his wounds anew.

Oh, my distressing words!
Solicitous and compassionate
I envisioned them to be.
Instead, they profane the peace
And silent pain he knew.

Why then,
Do I go on,
Saying these words
That harm instead of heal?

Agnes T. Pratt

I'M ONLY GOING TO TELL YOU ONCE

Shut up, and leave me be.
I'm lonely,
Can't you see?
Take your serpent slit-eyed grin
And squirm beneath a rock.
If you can recall what door
You slithered under to come in,
Use it when you slither out again.

––––––––

DEATH TAKES ONLY A MINUTE

Agonies of change
can be heard
in the lonely silence
of a single raindrop
bending a leaf downward.

All this is distant
and will fade further back
when my relatives assemble
to haggle over
the price of dying.

Agnes T. Pratt

EMPATHY

Our glances spin silver threads,
Weaving a web of closeness;
Catching, holding
A love too tenuous for words.
Woven and remembered
In silence, those hours
When time had something
To do with the moon.

    Stay, or flee
    As you must—
    Uncountable the ways
    We seek ourselves.
    I will keep
    The interwoven strands of you
    As I keep the enduring moon
    And its web of shadow.

FRAGMENTS OF SPRING

The earth is wondering,
a clear-eyed, awakened child.
Gray winter has melted,
and spring is bold
and laughing in emeralds.

From the shallow grave of winter
A purple hyacinth
Unfolds, bannering itself
Up and toward the treetops.

LAMENTATION

My sorrow cannot travel
To anywhere but myself.
What would I say
If I were there?
I could only push sympathies
Across the air
As I push salt
Across a table.

Agnes T. Pratt

HOPE TO KEEP

I keep nothing,
Nor can I glue together
Fragments of complacence
From the shattered prism
Of my emotions.
Fool who played with glass
Now has broken slivers of light
That hurt my hands
When I touch them.

———

SO QUICKLY CAME THE SUMMER

Night laid itself down beside the horizon,
The mountain wrapped itself in clouds,
Forest sighed through yellowing leaves
Hushed in mourning for dying spring.
So quickly came the summer
When spring departed, she left
A young boy strumming a guitar,
The moon sighing along its strings,
As he slowly walked down the hill.

Agnes T. Pratt

QUIETLY I SHOUT

A searching pain
As of a bladed edge
Knifes me to cry out.
Crying out, I laugh;
Jeering, taunting Pain
To cripple me!
True: not wound nor pain
Grieves me so much
As knowing the hand
That held the knife.

Phil George

Phillip William George, after two years in Vietnam and a long year on the California desert as an Army dental technician, is now a freshman at Ganzaga University. He is a member of the Nez Perce Nation at Lapwai, Washington.

He spent much of his early life with his maternal great-grandmother, living and learning the ways of his ancestors. He arrived at the Institute of American Indian Arts in the fall of 1964, a graduate of Coulee Dam High School. He was a well-known traditional Indian dance champion of the Pacific Northwest. His art interests were in traditional costuming, music, dance, and writing.

Phil and the dance club of which he was president performed before national and international dignitaries in Washington. His poetry was read before Congress and translated into many languages for use on the Voice of America broadcasts. His poetry and prose have been widely published by educational and trade publishers.

After Phil's eighth birthday, his "real" name, given him at birth by his great-grandmother, was officially bestowed with feasts and ceremonies. Relatives and friends attended from the Colville, Spokane, Yakima, Warm Springs, Umatilla, Flathead, and Rocky Boy reservations.

Lah-peh-ya-low-ett, the name of his great-grandfather, refers to two white swans gliding above still waters, symbolic of beauty, grace, purity, and peace. At the naming ceremony, Phil's Grandfather Seth explained the history of his father's sacred name.

"Lahpehyalowett lived across from the Palouse grasslands, east from the Kamiah valley. *Kamiah-pa* means 'the green valley with clear waters flowing through.' Lewis and Clark named the river Clearwater. The prairie adjoining pine forests allotted to Lahpehyalowett was perfect for horse raising. Because Lahpehyalowett owned hundreds of Appaloosa horses, the agent at Fort Lapwai named him Phillip, which means in Greek 'lover of horses.'"

PROVISO

After my wake, oh people of my lodge,
Place a drum upon my chest
And lay me on a travois—
An ancient, gentle travois.
In the dawn, not eventide, I beg,
Take me far away.
        I'll drum.
        I'll sing.

Carry me in regalia of bygone days
Plumed by the morning breath of Appaloosas,
Across the meadow of the camas,
Through satin dew upon Wallowa's shadow,
There leave me far away.
        I'll drum.
        I'll sing.

Hold me without bruising, as in embrace,
Carpeted on palms of loving hands.
Move through the camps from west to east,
For my sun rises, does not set,
And lifts me far away.
        I'll drum.
        I'll sing.

BATTLE WON IS LOST

They said, "You are no longer a lad."
   I nodded.
They said, "Enter the council lodge."
   I sat.
They said, "Our lands are at stake."
   I scowled.
They said, "We are at war."
   I hated.
They said, "Prepare red war symbols."
   I painted.
They said, "Count coups."
   I scalped.
They said, "You'll see friends die."
   I cringed.
They said, "Desperate warriors fight best."
   I charged.
They said, "Some will be wounded."
   I bled.
They said, "To die is glorious."
   They lied.

Phil George

OLD MAN, THE SWEAT LODGE

"This small lodge is now alive,
The womb of our mother, Earth.
The blackness in which we sit,
The ignorance of our impure minds,
These burning stones are
The coming of a new life."
Near my heart I place his words.

Naked, like an infant at birth, I crouch,
Cuddled upon fresh straw and boughs.
Confessing, I recall all evil deeds.
For each sin I sprinkle water on fire-hot stones;
Their hissing is a special song and I know
The place from which Earth's seeds grow is alive.

Old Man, the Sweat Lodge heals the sick;
Brings good fortune to one deserving.
Sacred steam rises—vapor fills my very being—
My pores slime out their dross.
After chanting prayers to the Great Spirit,
I lift a blanket to the East;
Through this door dawns wisdom.

Cleansed, I dive into icy waters.
Pure, I rinse away unworthy yesterday.
"My son, walk straight in this new life.
Youth I help to retain in you.
Return soon. Visit an old one.
Now, think clean, feel clean, be happy."
I thank you, Old Man, the Sweat Lodge.

SONG OF A NEW CRADLEBOARD

Oh little one, while
You sleep,
Dream good dreams and
Grow straight.
The flower of love—
The rose's branch,
Protects you.
On this pine board,
The white, soft doeskin
Incases you.
Beneath your delicate body
The tree moss
Nestles you.
May love from the rose
Be yours.
May purity enfold
Your life.
My child, be brave in war,
Wise in the council lodge.
Straight as this board
Which I have made this day,
May you forever walk.

Phil George

CHILD REST

Crispy, salty, fry bread, smoked, dried, deer meat
And ice water from the nearby spring—
Great grandmother's midday meal.
I nap.

In her lap she takes beeswax, needle, beads—
Her red and yellow flower needs an afternoon of sewing.
She half whistles, half hums an old song for me.
I sleep.

Faithful as a forest doe Kautsa watches over me.
Her red and yellow flower blossoms, beadwork complete.
Now, continuous humming, tapping of her moccasined foot
     stops . . .
I awake.

NIGHT BLESSING

Sleep plays hide-and-seek with darkness.
In reverence
All earth stands, head bowed.
Long-needled evergreens cease to
Proclaim hushed hymns of awe.
Between praise stanzas,
Night birds pause to listen,
While sending their magnetic fragrance,
The sweetness for this royalty,
Spring flowers in carpet hues
Halt their prancing dance.
Stars shoot through space
To herald Full Moon's entrance.

Within my tepee
I cannot remain on robes and blankets.
Far out into the still of night,
My heart goes forth.
I must stand in honor, respect,
One beside tepee shadows
Gazing toward snow-capped mountains.
I turn to face the East,
Waiting to receive
Her blessing.
"Oh, Ruler of the Night,
May I so live that all I do in time
Is preparation for lasting peace."

Phil George

Soon Dawn's mystic gaze
Moves toward me,
Falling upon each creature.
I raise yearning arms
And stand naked
Within Her sacred view.
Devotion surges in me
Overflows my littleness
And I must praise
In song and dance.
I am clothed in joy.
I am warmed, protected.
Content, I sleep.

Phil George

AMBITION

This summer I shall
Return to our Longhouse
Hide beneath a feathered hat,
And become an Old Man.

Phil George

MAKE ME A MAN

Ah, my first-slain deer!
You were swift and sure,
But Grandfather's arrows,
Piercing straight,
Have met their mark.
Rejoice! Mother Earth's gift—
Your frisky life—is now returned.
In you I cup my palms
To drink your blood, rich-red,
Warm as the Sun noon-high.
Buck, make me a man.

Round my ankles, around again,
I will string black hooves.
May I dance your grace,
Bound through light-pintoed forests.
Her hands, soft and loving,
My Mother will prepare
Your velvet skin, quivering flesh.
Near your heart, still throbbing.
I partake and now become
Warm-hearted, strong, alert.
Buck, make me a man.

Phil George

MONUMENT IN BONE

The Sun and I
Now honor you,
Bleaching buffalo bones.
To Mother Earth
Return in dust.
I tilt your skull
Towards Sun Father—
Round like the
Never-ending circle.
Around your bones
Four times, I dance.
Rest, for none is waste.
I hungered for you;
Honor I now pay you.

———

SELF

Sun Father, you above me,
　　　Protect;
White Owls, you before me,
　　　Delay;
Earth Spirits, you about me,
　　　Instruct
That my innate self I may
　　　Fulfill.

Phil George

SHADOWS AND SONG

Through pine-black stilettos
I see the White Moon—glowing.
Following, pulling me back,
A silent shadow.

I feel someone watching:
"Who-hoo, Who-hoo,"
Scold night owls—encircling.

Beside a stream I delay my tracks.
Wallowa's heart impulse—
Her gushing, icy brooks
Sing to me a joyful song.

Warm-brown moccasins
Sound out drumbeats
As they pace ancient paths.

Grandfathers now are
Dust in life-giving soil;
Through purple-flowered fields
They hum melodies of old.

I run from this sad shadow,
Black and cold as night,
Toward a happy, swaying body.

Phil George

ASK THE MOUNTAINS

Here I stand
For centuries watching
Moccasined trails
Wear down into
Paved highways.
Innumerable winter snows
Have robed me and
My sister—
Mother Earth.
To this moist
Green valley,
The Land of Winding Waters—
I give the beauty of
Purple peaks pointing.
From long ago
I have towered—
Unafraid.
Guarding ancient
Bits of wisdom
Learned by men and creatures.
To all inhabitants of this
New Switzerland,
The Mighty One
Smiles sunshine—
Together in happiness
We protect, provide.
In gaiety, liberty,
I saw the Nez Perce
Freely worship.

Phil George

Pure as my
Glacial Waters,
Proud as the bull Elk
They lived—
Seeking to survive
Within my shadow.
I helped establish these
Intelligent, ritualistic
People—a powerful race.
I admire their
Love for life.
From tribal burial grounds,
I have seen
Peace die and
Violence invade.
I know all truth.
I am Wallowa of the
Blue Mountains.

UNTIL THEN

Beside the drums my dusty moccasins
     cannot be still.
The death song is sung but once.

OLD MAN'S PLEA

Am I happy or sad that I cry inside,
Whimpers unheard, my unseen?
Next season what relative, what friend
Will not be here to dance or sing
Beside old-time embers almost cold?

Let me live this Indian Night
And I will die tomorrow.

Phil George

MORNING BEADS

Into drops of crystal dew
Displayed upon a lily leaf,
I see tonight's desire.

One bead . . . another . . .
Trickles down, down;
Embellishing the camas stem.

With the Jeweler of the Dawn
Mother strings beads in sunrise hues
On moccasins I will wear tonight.

THROUGH DAWN'S PINK AURORA

Through dawn's
Pink aurora
A leaf sailed.
Skyward I
Opened my palms
And caught beauty.
I felt a year's
Happiness,
Inspiration,
Love,
Knowledge
When I touched
The dew-flecked leaf
That fell
This early morn.

Phil George

COYOTE'S NIGHT

This is Coyote's night
For skies are clear;
Crickets quit singing
So he must be near.
    Shh, sleep, Sister.

I can see his body
In a puppy-like squat,
There in the meadow—
A fool's hiding spot!
    Shh, sleep, Sister.

Embers still glow,
The fire will start;
Perhaps he may flee
If he really is smart.
    Shh, sleep, Sister.

Ah, here comes the moon.
We'll scare that dog . . .
(The fool is on me;
It is only a log!)
    Shh, sleep, Sister.